LA FLEUR DE LIS

Histories, Mysteries, Recipes & Mixologies
of the World's Most Enduring Symbol

Photos and Text by Morgan McCall Molthrop
Design and Foreword by Casey Delmont Johnson

www.fleur-de-lis.com

Published by
Barataria Communications
in collaboration with
Roux Brands dba Fleur-de-lis.com

Copyright 2015

All rights reserved. No part of this book may be reproduced in any form or by any means
without the prior written consent of the publisher, excepting brief quotes used in reviews.

Library of Congress, The United States of America

For Angela.

In memory of Angela Carville Fluker. A portion of the proceeds of this book will be used to inspire creativity and economic growth in communities around the globe. Like the fleur de lis itself, we plant seeds of creativity in young minds and bring hope to desolate places.

FOREWORD

I was raised in the Mississippi Delta in South Louisiana. The fleur de lis was so ubiquitous that I was fairly oblivious to it. When I was tapped to become Director of Fleur-de-Lis.com, I inherited the design of our products. Market research showed that fleur merchandise was on its way out. But there was something that made me question the experts. I would come to realize that the fleur is one of the most enduring symbols in history.

One small book could never reveal all the mysteries of the fleur de lis. Our goal was to provide an overview of its influence in this Southern realm, to trace its oft-disputed history, and to offer ways for you to enjoy the fleur de lis as we do: through food, music, cocktails, and spirituality.

To accomplish this we could not help but delve into the "occult." While I was designing my first line, I found the fleur as a glyph for "Ruler" or "Lord" in Mesoamerican art. Meanwhile, thousands of miles away, in another delta, the Egyptians were using similar symbols in temples and hieroglyphs. How could two great civilizations adopt the same symbol for the same thing?

Egypt has always held its sway with me. The nation-state was split into Upper and Lower parts - ruled seperately - before Narmer, a powerful warlord, united the kingdom. Egyptian rulers, from then on, included the combined symbology of both the lotus and the papyrus.

The fleur's plant-like origins contain three upper and three lower portions. They create a spiritual symbology similar to the Chinese yin and yang. The three upper petals are reflected by three smaller downward-facing petals. A fleur is not complete without these aspects. Seen as roots or nourishment, the lower reaches of the fleur conjure darker meanings. The larger portion, above, however, remains in the light. It is the flower in full blossom - nurtured, fed, reflected, accentuated.

Just like the fleur de lis, the State Capitol in Baton Rouge held little significance for me. It was constructed for Louisiana's Kingfish, Governor Huey P. Long, a man who held almost absolute power over the state. Many thought Long would have become President had he not been assassinated *in the building he had commissioned*.

The Egyptian Renaissance friezes on the building are full of "predecessor" symbology. When I encountered them recently by accident, (though I don't believe these things are ever accidental) my jaw dropped. What was Long trying to say?

The Bourbon fleur is often associated with New Orleans. Long, from a poor family in rural Louisiana, styled himself as a "man of the people." He coined the phrase: "Every man a king." Long was looked down upon by snooty New Orleans power-brokers who knew he was trying to break their cabal.

LOTUS AND PAPYRUS

By harkening back to pre-fleur imagery, Long was effectively using earlier symbols. Napoleon had done the same thing in France when he adopted the bee over the Bourbon fleur. The Emporer replaced the Bourbon kings and erased their symbol. However, he was clever enough to know that the bee is also associated with the fleur and, in many ways, an earlier version of it. Long was reclaiming the fleur and conjuring the power of Egypt to trump the Francophile elites of New Orleans.

Perhaps. One can come to many conclusions about a symbol like the fleur. Like all mysteries, this may just be a coincidence. But consider this: The capitol of Louisiana rises to the same height as the Great Pyramid of Egypt.

As Roux Brands reinvents itself to appeal to a new generation intrigued by the fleur de lis, I hope that you enjoy our attempt to provide a few clues into the influence the symbol has held since the dawn of civilization.

Casey Delmont Johnson
Director, fleur-de-lis.com

(Photo: Russian Academy of Sciences)
Perphaps the first fleur de lis: The Pharoah Narmer used the lotus of Upper Egypt and the papyrus of Lower Egypt to create a fleur-like design that would reinforce his primacy over a combined powerhouse that would become one of the world's greatest civilizations.

The Gulf South's Most Regal (and roguish) Symbol

Barataria Communications for Roux Brands
www.fleur-de-lis.com

The origin of the fleur is a mystery. Related symbols are found in ancient civilizations predating the Hellenized world into which Christ was born. Fleur-like imagery is found in Egyptian hieroglyphics, Assyrian sculpture and Mesoamerican art. French kings in Medieval times adopted the symbol. English nobility, laying claim to France, followed suit. The sixth son of an English nobleman bears the fleur de lis on his coat of arms. A version of the fleur was the stamp of powerful, commercial Florence, the nexus of the Italian Renaissance.

By the time the fleur de lis arrived in the New World, it was an unmistakable symbol of the powerful European realms and their emissaries. Emblazoned on heraldic shields, worked into jeweled crowns, tiaras, and scepters, the fleur meant something to those who wore it and to those presented it in the pageantry of state. The fleur was borne into the American colonies on the crest of Virginia, England's tobacco-rich prize.

Fleurs de lis on the flag of colonial New France - modern-day Canada - snapped in brisk North Atlantic winds. When French-Canadian explorers descended the Mississippi in 1682 to claim the great waterway and its tributaries for the Bourbon Dynasty's most famous monarch, the Sun King at Versailles, they brought the fleur to "seal the deal."

To Louisiana, christened for King Louis XIV, magistrates, militiamen, and merchants brought the fleur de lis. To Gulf Coast outposts in Biloxi, Mobile and Gulfport, the fleur arrived with settlers who hoped to start a new life. The fleur was especially important to the King's Regent, the Duke d'Orleans, when New Orleans, his namesake, was founded in 1718. The Company of the West, given the monopoly to commercialize the city by the Duke, incorporated the fleur into its logo. With corporate emissaries came enslaved Africans, branded with the fleur to show that they were "property" of the royally-approved venture.

When the Spanish Crown transferred to the French House of Bourbon, the dynastic fleur was synthesized into Spanish symbology. Subsequently, the fleur arrived on the white beaches of Florida, sailed into colorful Caribbean ports, and was carried inland through the mountains and deserts of continental New Spain.

In the New World, the fleur de lis proclaimed "Old World" regal power and planted the seeds for budding commercial enterprises.

Joan of Arc, the "Maid of Orleans" carried the fleur de lis on her banner as she led an army. Today her statue stands on a verdant azalea island in the Vieux Carre, a gilded gift from France, still considered the "mother country" by some locals.

Louisiana's vast territories once included land from the Rocky Mountains to the Appalachians. Vestiges of empirical power in the form of the fleur today exist in the symbology of the former French outpost of St. Louis, where the upper petals have come to symbolize the meeting of three rivers. In once-French Detroit, Chevrolet sports cars adopted the fleur de lis. The Canadian coat of arms still bears the fleur. But the fleur's impression has been stamped most indelibly in Louisiana.

In Louisiana and along the Gulf Coast the seductive symbol is cherished by hundreds of thousands. For denizens of Louisiana's cities, swamps and bayous - and for neighbors along the stretch of coast between Pass Christian, Mississippi to Pensacola, Florida - historic memories, family ties, steamy subtropical weather, and the abundance of the Delta create a unique culture that falls under a symbol more deeply ingrained than any other: the fleur de lis. The lifestyle in these parts is more Caribbean than American.

The fleur de lis exists in the dreams of a people who share a love of place and a sense of history. These dreams vest in the mysteries of a land where children dig for buried pirate treasure; where moss drips from ancient oaks; where outdoor festivals erupt on weekdays; where magnolias blossoms fill the air with sweet perfume; where shrimp boats spread their wings; where brothers delicately-balance pirogues through the opaque mazes of backyard bayous; where an order of oysters-on-the-half and jambalaya proclaim that it is Friday afternoon; and where the score includes the drumbeat of Senegambia, the very roots of jazz. Whether in response to disaster or during grand celebrations, the fleur is present as a symbol of resilience, pride and home.

The Bible references the lily; it is found in the art and architecture of the Near East. European irises and lily flowers were considered related until modern classification systems placed them in different families. By then the fleur de lis, which translates to "lily flower," was a stylized "brand." The French fleurs de lis look more like Gallic irises than lilies. Some suggest the symbol is a bee. Scholars continue to debate ancient roots. But when new arrivals to Louisiana and along the Gulf Coast found a profusion of irises blooming, they took note: it was, one settler proclaimed, "as if the royal House of Bourbon had sprinkled the landscape with its divine symbol to stake [its] claim to the new territory."

The fleur arrived on Gulf shores as a "known quantity" with the first explorers and, later, with the first governmental and military infrastructure. It was brought by "company men" to consummate contracts made in the new colonies. The Company of the West, a primary developer of the Gulf Coast and New Orleans, used the fleur in correspondences with the legal authority vested in it by the King of France.

Property was stamped and branded. The fleur was seared into the flesh of escaped prisoners and enslaved Africans. While this has lent recent controvery to its use as a local symbol, the fleur's African roots, perhaps, create an alternative interpretation - providing the kind of balance that the fleur seems to continually symbolize.

No matter how you interpret the fleur, one thing's certain: if you were in Louisiana, you belonged to "the realm."

Everyone, including the royals, belonged to the realm. The realm was an integral part of the "universal" Catholic Church. Fleur de lis designs adorned Christian monuments for centuries. The idea of separation of church and state was unthinkable to their "Catholic Majesties" of France and Spain. As such, the fleur de lis was built into - if not literally carried into - the Catholic churches and cathedrals of the New World.

The three petaled flower also represents the Holy Trinity. The symbol is associated with Mary, Jesus' mother. However, the alternating three lower petals at the base create a "reflection" that endorses the upper structure and prompts further contemplation. Some numerologists and believers in the occult suggest other meanings of spirituality - perhaps not as pure as Mary. Some believe there are angelic undertones to the symbol. Some think it represents the ultimate Fallen Angel.

In New Orleans Vodou, the fleur provides an apt symbol for the idea that the world of the living is reflected in the spiritual realm. In fact, many of the slaves and prisoners branded with the fleur de lis would become masters and princes of the new colony.

Napoleon (not a Bourbon but one whose emblem - the bee - is, according to many scholars, an early version of the fleur) planned an extensive French empire in the New World to be ruled from New Orleans. The long, often perilous trip from France to New Orleans required a "pit stop" for vessels to take on water and supplies. A slave rebellion on the designated refueling island, sugar cane-rich San Domingue (modern-day Haiti), thwarted the emperor's plot. Subsequently, Napoleon sold Louisiana - a third of the North American continent - to the young United States in 1803.

Ironically, the influx of wealthy plantation owners, merchants, free people of color and pirates fleeing the Haitian slave revolt doubled the size of New Orleans and reinforced its Caribbean flare just as the Americans attempted to impose Puritanical values on a Catholic population. The San Domingans brought luxurious tastes, the *en vogue* Bonapartist bee and the Bourbon Dynastic fleur, with them. As Napoleon fell, so did the bee. But the fleur - which had been with the city from the start - lasted.

Unable to commercially or socially conquer the close-knit, exotic Caribbean society they inherited, the Americans created their own more sober "Yankee" city upriver of the French Quarter in Faubourg St. Marie and the Garden District. The native Creoles continued to live as they had in downriver neighborhoods.

To say the two groups disliked one another would be an understatement. A full blown cultural warfare for the "heart" of New Orleans was underway. Meanwhile, an economic boom ushered in an era of tremendous wealth for both societies. Currency printed and coined in Louisiana included the fleur de lis.

The rarified Creoles first denied the reality of American ascendancy. Like the Spanish overlords before, the Americans, they believed, might be temporary caretakers, to be tolerated - barely - while they went about "business as usual." Many were quoted as saying: "Give 'les Américaines' a few hot summers here and they will leave or adjust to our ways." Adjust they did.

Today during Mardi Gras, the fleur de lis accompanies royalty in a form incomprehensible to Americans in other parts of the nation. Here "royalty" flourishes in a country that long ago cut the cord with king and queen. Here, pretend kings and queens dance at balls, present debutante courts, "create tableau" and grace theatrical thrones. The fleur de lis is woven into the pageantry.

The fact that Americans who moved into French territory adopted many of the local customs is not surprising. At first reluctant, Americans who made New Orleans their home began to mimic French style. Even priggish American ladies couldn't resist the latest Parisian fashions. French style transferred to the American nouveau riche. Americans even began to celebrate a medieval Catholic holiday that had been a masking tradition in the city since its founding.

When a significant influx of Irish and Sicilian Italians began to change the city's demographics in the latter part of the 19th century, the competing European Creole and upper crust American societies that had once battled for social dominance collapsed into each other's arms like lovers. Distinctions between Catholic and Protestant were less important than strict distinctions between race and class. By then they had been "at it" for so long that their customs almost mirrored one another's.

Americans in Louisiana would come to embrace the fleur de lis when European Creoles joined wealthy Americans to create social organizations that advanced political and business agendas. All of this was part of a plan to maintain control in an uneasy postbellum city. As Carnival's overlords, the Creolized Americans ruled over a "chaotic city" that seemed to require social order- especially on Carnival Day when "Chaos" reigned.

The pecking order changed, the caste system that had been in place for almost two centuries evolved, and a new Mardi Gras emerged that used the trappings of French royalty to validate a new "American" regime. On the crowns and scepters of Southern "kings and queens," the fleur de lis lived on.

Jambalaya

INGREDIENTS

1 1/2 pounds smoked sausage
1 pound andouille sausage
1/2 pound tasso*
6 skinless, boneless chicken thighs
4 cups trinity**
Salt, pepper and creole seasoning
1 tablespoon chopped fresh thyme
1 teaspoon chili powder
1 diced tomato
3 cups beef consommé
1/4 bunch chopped parsley
1/2 cup chopped green onions
3 cups white rice

PREPARATION

Cut meats into bitesize portions then combine in a large dutch oven. Season with salt, pepper, and creole or cajun seasoning. Brown very well. Add the cajun trinity and sauté together for 15 minutes. Follow with the beef consommé, stirring in tomato, green onions and remaining spices. Cook for another 15 minutes on medium-high heat, stirring often. Add 3 cups water and 3 cups white rice. Cover and cook until the rice is tender. Finally, remove the lid until and allow the mixture to become fluffy.

**

*Tasso is cajun for a lean cut of cured pork.

**The cajun trinity is a version of *mirepoix*, a French base of roughly cut vegetables. In this case the trinity contains a mixture of onion, bell pepper and celery proportioned to taste.

In 1762, in a secret treaty between cousins of the House of Bourbon, Louis XV of France ceded Louisiana - the entire central portion of North America - to Carlos III of Spain. The Bourbon symbol would, then, remain a symbol of power in Louisiana throughout its colonial period.

Spanish Governors with the fleur de lis prominently displayed on their coats of arms arrived to find a population that had eked out an existence without much assistance from "the powers that be." Not appreciating new regal authority, the colonists rebelled and proclaimed their independence. Spain eventually exerted its control, but after two hard-fought generations in an unforgiving, hurricane-prone, diseased, swampy backwater, the survivalist native Creole population was averse to change. Ultimately, Spanish bureaucrats did more "blending" than controlling.

Culturally, however, Spanish influence became important in music, architecture and food. Brass bands and African drumbeats would be foundational to jazz. Fires during the late 18th century created the necessity to rebuild the original "French Quarter" into a Spanish Caribbean town of substance. The master plan called for a "fire-proof" city with built-in carriageways that led to patios. To avoid fires in the main house, food preparation was done in back slave quarters by African cooks. Under the direction of Spanish senoras, paella - with a pinch of this and some local fare - emerged as jambalaya. A new dish was brought to a table already set with the fleur de lis.

The Merieult House in the French Quarter is home to the Historic New Orleans Collection.

New Orleans is considered the most Catholic city in the US. Its liberal use in Catholic churches and St. Louis Cathedral provides insight into the seamlessness that existed between church and state.

While many believe St. Louis Cathedral is a French structure, it was built as a Spanish mission. The original wood structure was destroyed by the Great Fire of 1788. Restoration and revisions to the original building, including the main tower and steeples to replace domes, resulted in the iconic amalgamation that one associates with New Orleans today. Fleur de lis were built into the building, painted on the ceiling and used in stained glass. After all, Saint Louis was the only French king to be sainted. His symbol? The fleur de lis.

The Spanish colonies along the the Gulf provided refuge for thousands of people who wanted to remain Catholic and start a new life. The people who settled French and Spanish territory here were familiar with the fleur and its divine, if not noble, implications. Islenos from the Canary Islands, and 'Cajuns' from Acadia brought fleur de lis with them. The fleur was part of Catholic symbolism brought by Irish immigrants fleeing English repression.

Enslaved Africans were forced to be Catholic and attend mass. Because the city had a large population of free people of color, the church provided opportunities for devout Catholics within its infrastructure. Henriette Delille created the Sisters of the Holy Family to care for orphans and the education of black Catholics. Today the order's parish church displays the fleur de lis.

Perhaps the most famous woman in the world to wear the Bourbon fleur de lis was Marie Antoinette. Misunderstood, but surely a willful personality that attracted attention, Marie Antoinette came to symbolize all that was "excessive" with the French monarchical world into which she married. Of Austro-Hungarian birth, she was betrothed to the French Dauphin who would become King Louis XVI. The king (the same one who ceded Louisiana to Spain) was more interested in making locks than governing the nation. The people of France, suffering from the impact of the ultimate top-down economy, blamed royalty for their suffering. They targeted Marie Antoinette. Eventually, it was "off with their heads" and the fleur de lis necklaces that graced them.

Today Marie Antoinette has become a symbol herself, associated with the luxury, beauty, frivolity and corruption of the declining court at Versailles. While the Bourbon Dynasty would briefly be resurrected, with the murder of the royals the fleur de lis came to symbolize a past from which revolutionaries would distance themselves.

In Louisiana, the shock of the revolution, the American takeover and the subsequent immigration of wealthy San Domingans resulted in too much change, too fast. This created nostalgia for a more secure, if not noble past. Many French fleeing the revolution ended up in New Orleans to save their own necks. Royalists and Bonapartists adapted to the city and kept up with the latest Parisian fashions. But they held on to their fleurs de lis. By now the symbol had become unique to a region that was - culturally - in danger of being overcome by Americans who were flooding in every day. The fleur was the symbol of resistance for the French and Caribbean citizens against a new nation with a value set and customs that were foreign to them.

At the same time, the fleur took on new meanings to people of African descent. People from West Africa had seen the symbol from their own continent in art and architecture. By the time many enslaved had gained their freedom in the rather fluid Louisiana society, the fleur was adopted into the Afro-Catholic synthesis religion that was prominently practiced until the late 19th century.

Vodou would go "underground" (just like the three lower "petals" of the fleur) for a century only to emerge in full force after Hurricane Katrina. The fleur de lis as a symbol of resilience and resistance remained in tact. This became fully apparent when the International Shrine of Marie Laveau was ceremonially dedicated in 2015 by Vodou Priestess Sallie Ann Glassman.

21 • THE TWO MARIES

Arguably the most famous woman in New Orleans history - Marie Laveau - worked tirelessly alongside the Catholic priests to serve yellow fever victims and comfort prisoners on Death Row. Though a mystic leader of African non-violent resistance during repressive times, the "Voodoo Queen" was baptized in the Catholic Church and buried in the Catholic cemetery.

Ms. Glassman, an indoctrinated priestess who practices in New Orleans today, says that she incorporated the fleur into her religious symbology - or "veves" - for Marie Laveau after Katrina. "I felt that the fleur both symbolized the powerful resilience of the people of New Orleans and their long-time capacity to create beauty out of adversity. I incorporated the fleur de lis into the International Shrine of Marie Laveau's mosaic design for the same reason."

THE DEAD VOUDOU QUEEN

MARIE LAVEAU'S PLACE IN THE HISTORY OF NEW-ORLEANS.

THE EARLY LIFE OF THE BEAUTIFUL YOUNG CREOLE—THE PROMINENT MEN WHO SOUGHT HER ADVICE AND SOCIETY—HER CHARITABLE WORK—HOW SHE BECAME AN OBJECT OF MYSTERY.

NEW-ORLEANS, June 21.—Marie Laveau, the "Queen of the Voudous," died last Wednesday at the advanced age of 98 years. To the superstitious creoles Marie appeared as a dealer in the black arts and a person to be dreaded and avoided. Strange stories were told of the rites performed by the sect of which Marie was the acknowledged sovereign. Many old residents asserted that on St. John's night, the 24th of June, the Voudou clan had been seen in deserted places joining in wild, weird dances, all the participants in which were perfectly nude. The Voudous were thought to be invested with supernatural powers, and men always concerned her, and she eagerly s[ought] news of his movements. She was proud o[f her] interview with Lafayette, who, when he v[isited] New-Orleans, over 50 years ago, called a[t her] house and printed a warm kiss [on] her forehead at parting. Marie Laveau [was] one of the band of colored people [who] escorted to the tomb, long since disma[ntled] in the old Catholic cemetery, the remains o[f the] scarred and grizzly French General, Hum[bert]. The hero of Castelbar was often a visitor at [her] house, and she was rich with anecdotes con[cern]ing him. The pious Father Antoine, of bl[essed] memory, met her often at the bedside of the c[lients] she to ease their sufferings during their las[t mo]ments in this life, and he to give hope of salv[ation] in the life beyond.

Marie Laveau, one of the most wonderful w[omen] who ever lived, passed peaceably away. [Her] daughter, Mme. Philomel Legendre, the only [sur]vivor of all Capt. Glapion's children, who poss[esses] many of the characteristics of her mother[, and] Mme. Legendre's two pretty daughters, minis[tered] to the old lady's last wants. She died wi[thout] a struggle, with a smile lighting up her shri[veled] features. She was interred in her family tom[b by] the side of Capt. Glapion, in the old St. [Louis] Cemetery, and with her is buried the most th[rilling] portion of the unwritten records of Louisiana[. Al]though Marie Laveau's history has been very [much] sought after, it has never been published. [Cable] has endeavored to portray her in the charac[ter of] Palmyre, in his novel of the "Grandissimes," [the] secrets of her life, however, could only be ob[tained]

The fleur was literally built into the French Quarter and stuccoed into government buildings throughout the French colonial region. The Governor's mansion near the river, his home in what is now the Central Business District, the cathedral, the military barracks and the magazines that would become the first dance halls all sported the fleur de lis.

Inside modest Creole cottages and on the doors of "shotgun" houses, the fleur became an ornamental necessity. Fireplaces, stained glass windows, cast iron fences and above-ground-tombs used the fleur to enhance the elegance of interior and exterior spaces, as well as to associate the living - and dead - with the "divine."

Even the simplicity of Greek Revival styles popular during the "Gilded Age" of ante-bellum Gulf societies could not be constrained in a place where half of the millionaires in the United States now lived. The trappings of royalty were too tempting, even to the new Protestant immigrants into French Louisiana. The fleur de lis migrated - in the form of fabrics and wallpaper - into "American" plantations upriver and beyond.

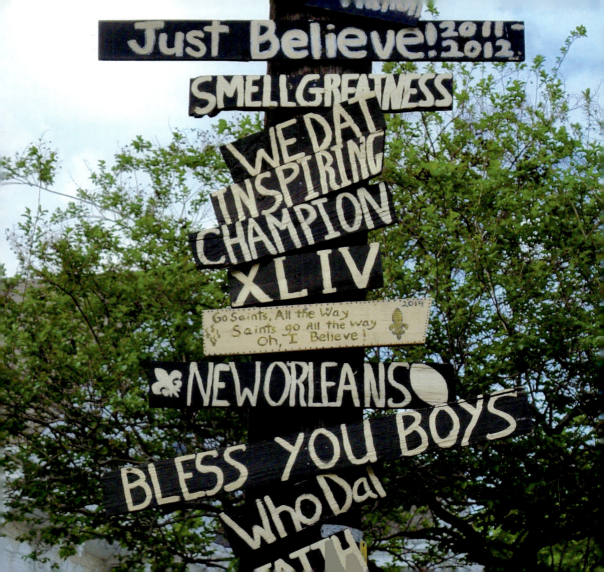

Doors have always held symbolic meaning. Entering a palace, temple, noble home or a simple hut often meant following certain protocols. The god Janus - the two-headed God - was used in Roman doorways to see in and out. Perhaps no city in America has more photogenic - or more photographed - doorways than New Orleans.

Simple doors from 19th century working class shotguns are often made of wood with a window and architectural detail surrounding it. Quite often, a fleur de lis will grace the door or the mantel above a portal. On the opposite side of town, massive leaded glass windows in the Garden District and Uptown contain patterns that often include the fleur de lis. "Wreaths" sport the fleur de lis on homes during Mardi Gras.

Because of the tropical climate, porches in New Orleans and surrounding communities represent an "extra room" where news and gossip can be spread between neighbors. Decorating porches and doorways as if they were extensions of the house is not only common - it's expected. Throughout the Gulf South and in Western and Northern Louisiana, the fleur can be found on porches as bric-a-brac or flags. The fleur claims the space as a portion of local pride - a sign that the people who live here "live here."

New Orleans and New York were once the most sporting cities in America. What New Orleans had going for it was a sense of "joie de vivre" - joy of life - for which the French had become famous. The legalized brothels in Storyville were famous sexual circuses in grand mansions built by the most famous architects of the day, owned by local government officials and run by famous Madames.

New Orleans' was home to a dozen race tracks, countless gaming houses and more bars and taverns per capita than any city on American soil: a statistic it continues to hold to this day.

In a "Gilded Age," the fleur would be printed on playing cards, etched in wine glasses, painted on ladies' fans, worn on broaches, pinned on "tignons" and fashioned into extravagant wigs and hats. Long white gloves might have embroidered fleurs at the buttons. Men's shoe buckles, vests, cigar boxes and carriages were emblazoned with the fleur de lis.

The fleur would not only become a symbol of the region, it would be incorporated as a symbol of many of the sporting teams and societies of the day. Today the fleur is the symbol of the New Orleans Saints. Few NFL fans understand that the symbol on the side of a helmet is, in actuality, a royal dynastic symbol. Or that the Saints refer to the Catholic Saints. The Saints may not win every game, but it doesn't hurt to have King and God on your side.

27 • THE SPORTING LIFE

In colonial Louisiana letters were often sealed in wax and stamped. French symbols were used in communications, commercial documents and government mandates. During the Spanish period, French correspondences between families in the Gulf colonies and their relatives abroad continued. The fleur became widespread in the American South, especially along the river, as cotton and sugar commerce blossomed.

The French and Spanish planter class - the owners of plantations on the river and Bayou St. John - sought every opportunity to associate themselves with nobility. In New Orleans, that meant dressing the part and "acting noble." Using the fleur de lis, a symbol of power, was a natural choice for *nouveau riche* looking to put their oft-ignoble past behind them.

In the Victorian era, long letters were shared between families and loved ones. Especially prevalent were letters among families impacted by the American Civil War. This included correspondences between French family members separated by the conflict: those who stayed behind to protect property and those who fled to France to wait out the war. By then the fleur was commonly embossed into paper sold at the stationer's shop.

Mail slots and boxes appeared in the 19th century. The fleur was cast into the first boxes in New Orleans to contain US Mail.

31 • MEROVINGIAN KINGS

The fleur de lis is directly associated with French monarchy in the 12th century. In one legend, King Clovis followed the yellow lilies - irises, to us - to help find a shallow ford in a river, allowing his army to cross and defeat his enemies.

The fleur de lis transferred well into a craze for cast iron that began in the Victorian Age, when the Baroness Pontalba built chic apartment complexes modeled after the latest Parisian styles on the Place de Armes. As part of a master plan to "reinvigorate" the Creole Quarter where she had grown up, she also helped raise the funds to landscape the park leading to the Cathedral from the river and placed the iconic statue of Andrew Jackson before it. Today fleur-like symbols are found in the antique fences and gates that help define the boundaries of the region.

The fleur is so common in the Gulf South that it is literally "hidden in plain sight." We eat pastries decorated with the design and drink cocktails named after it. Take a look around you next time you're in Louisiana. You can order a fleur de lis gumbo, drink a fleur de lis cocktail, listen to jazz that is named for the symbol and decorate your home in fleur de lis prints and patterns.

But you don't have to travel to New Orleans to play this game. This book contains several hidden fleurs. While the images are quite often self-explanatory, look twice. Or maybe three times. We've included clues that reflect the text and created a puzzle. For hints, go to our website at www.fleur-de-lis.com/thebook and maybe you will find the mysteries we've peppered throughout these pages.

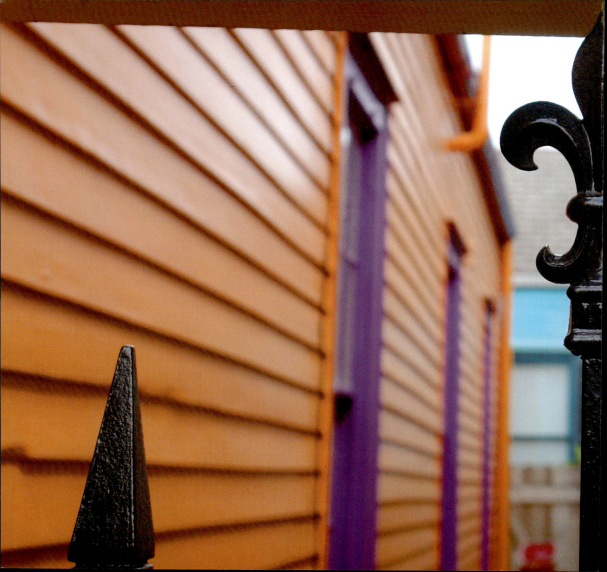

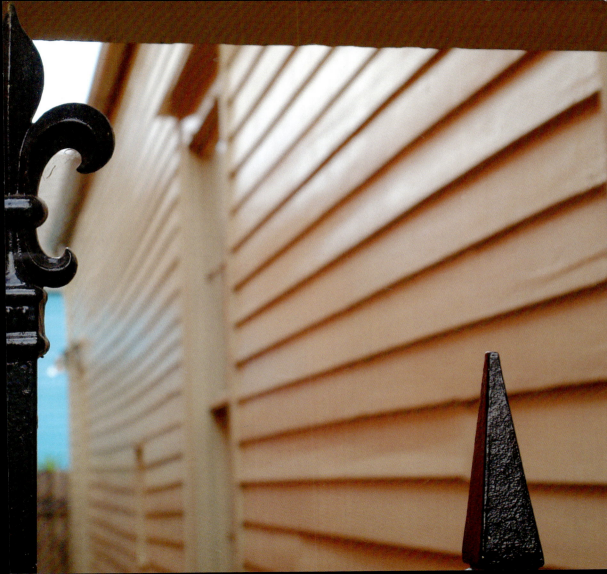

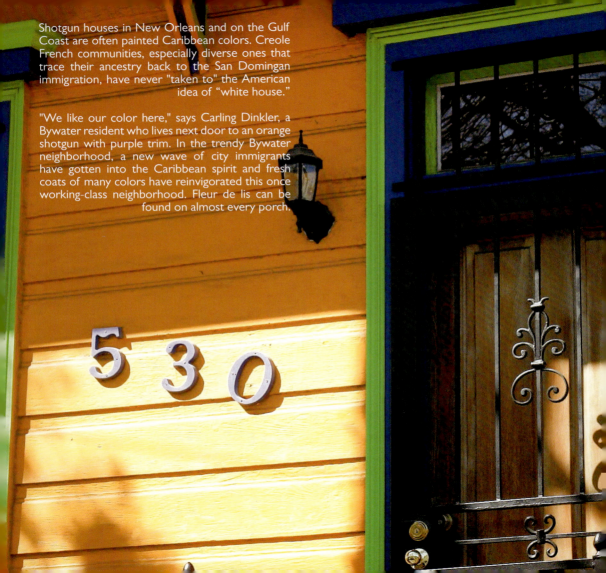

Shotgun houses in New Orleans and on the Gulf Coast are often painted Caribbean colors. Creole French communities, especially diverse ones that trace their ancestry back to the San Domingan immigration, have never "taken to" the American idea of "white house."

"We like our color here," says Carling Dinkler, a Bywater resident who lives next door to an orange shotgun with purple trim. In the trendy Bywater neighborhood, a new wave of city immigrants have gotten into the Caribbean spirit and fresh coats of many colors have reinvigorated this once working-class neighborhood. Fleur de lis can be found on almost every porch.

Hospitality: a tradition in the American South. The Mississippi River was the Internet of its day. Travel up the river from New Orleans helped spread genteel society throughout the region and into cities like St. Louis. For instance, the term "belle of the ball" comes from the French word for beautiful. Balls, a New Orleans tradition since 1718, would become the height of antebellum fashion. Margaret Mitchell's fictional Scarlett O'Hara would be remembered as a "Southern Belle" long after this era passed.

Rich details of Louisiana's "high life" including the fleur de lis would become part of respectable society everywhere. Grand hotels would fold their napkins into a fleur de lis design that was introduced at the St. Louis Hotel in the French Quarter and perfected at the St. Charles Hotel in the American District.

Every year New Orleans hosts "Tales of the Cocktail," an unconventional convention that attracts bar owners and mixologists from around the world. They converge on the Crescent City to test new drink recipes and share heritage stories and legends surrounding spirits and the mixers that transform them. It's no surprise that at Muriel's restaurant on Jackson Square, the "Fleur de Lis cocktail" is a constant favorite. Here's how to make one:

Muriel's Fleur de Lis Cocktail

1 1/4	ounces Stoli Raspberry Vodka
1/2	ounce Chambord
1/4	ounce orange juice
1/4	ounce pineapple juice

Pour all ingredients over ice into a cocktail shaker and shake. Strain over 1/4-ounce sparkling wine or champagne into a martini glass. Garnish with an orange slice.

The first cocktail was created by a San Domingan pharmacist who immigrated to New Orleans in the early 19th century and opened up shop on Royal Street. Peychaud invented bitters to settle an upset stomach. He served the elixir with Sazerac brandy in an egg cup. Americans could not pronounce the French word for egg cup - *coquetier*. They simply called it a "cock tail." The Sazerac cocktail was born. Upriver, the first cocktail party in recorded history was thrown by Mrs. Julia Walsh in St. Louis. As her 50 guests were served libations before noon, we would have called them "eye openers." Though *tres Américain*, we like to think that Mrs. Walsh decorated in French style with the fleur de lis.

During a recent interview with Leah Chase, the city's most famous Creole chef, she said that in Creole society, the women did most of the cooking. She insinuated - with a conspiratorial smile - that, perhaps, the best way to deal with a man was through his stomach - whether she wanted to get to his heart or not.

Heartburn aside, a culture can be defined by its cuisine. Some believe that Louisiana's cuisine is the only truly indigenous fare in the United States. The combination of Native American elements (sassafras leaves that make up the file in gumbo, for instance); the creation of French confections by using local brown sugar and pecans for pralines; okra seeds brought by the West Africans in their hair, cooked by the enslaved; pastas and sauces from Sicilian Italians; and fusion seafood dishes from the more recent Vietnamese immigrants create a unique cuisine which Chef John Folse refers to as "the bounty of several continents."

Food and spirits continue to be essential elements of Gulf Coast culture. Crawfish are boiled in big pots, some of which bear a logo that incorporates the fleur de lis. Restaurants use the symbol in their signs, on their plates, utensils and on the menus. The food itself is often named for the fleur.

Patisseries prided themselves in creating unique delicacies for the palates of the "Gilded Age." Bakers placed fleurs de lis on petits four and sugar cookies. Today beignets, cupcakes and king cakes bear the royal stamp. Like our Monday tradition of red beans and rice - legendarily cooked on 'wash day' when the beans can soak while the laundry is done.

Gumbo

1 cup vegetable oil
1 cup all-purpose flour
1 large onion, diced
1/2 cup chopped celery
1/2 cup chopped green bell pepper
3/4 cup okra
1 diced tomato
1/4 bunch chopped parsley
8 blue crabs with claws, cleaned
2 lbs large gulf shrimp, peeled
Salt, pepper and creole seasoning
1 tablespoon liquid crab boil
2 1/2 cups cooked white rice

In a gumbo pot, combine oil and flour and cook over medium-high heat. Stir constantly. This creates the roux. After the roux turns dark brown, add the trinity* (cajun for onion, bell pepper and celery - "holy trinity" also includes garlic). Sauté for 15 minutes adding salt, pepper, and creole seaoning.

In another pot, combine prepared shrimp and prepared crabs in enough water to cover them only. Add liquid crab boil, and boil the seafood for 15 mins. Cut heat and pour 1/2 of this seasoned crab and shrimp stock into the roux, leaving the remainder in the seafood pot.

Add tomato and parsley then cook over medium-low an additional 25 minutes. Next, add seafood and remaining stock. Cook for 15 minutes. Follow with okra. Cook the gumbo an additional 15 minutes. Serve over cooked rice.

Red Beans

1 lb dried red beans
3 tablespoons bacon grease
1 cup chopped tasso**
1/2 pound smoked sausage
2 cups holy trinity
Salt, pepper and creole seasoning
3 bay leaves
2 teaspoons thyme
1/4 bunch chopped parsley
10 cups chicken stock
2 1/2 cups cooked white rice

Soak the red beans in water overnight. Afterwards, drain and add chicken stock. Cook on medium until the beans begin to get tender. Then add holy trinity*, bacon grease and seasonings. Stir in prepared, bitesize meats. Cook together on medium-low for one hour. Stir the beans occasionally in order to create a creamy texture. Serve over cooked rice.

Recipes compliments of a real cajun mom, Bonita Cotton.

*The cajun trinity is a version of *mirepoix,* a French base of roughly cut vegetables. In this case the trinity contains a mixture of onion, bell pepper and celery proportioned to taste. The cajun holy trinity includes garlic.

**Tasso is a lean cut of cured pork.

RECIPES [AGAINST] DISASTER

The fleur is everywhere. It has many meanings. Some believe it retains power. Others believe it is a primary archetypal symbol. Some believe the fleur is one of the most sacred symbols in the world.

"If every society from the dawn of man has used one iteration of the symbol in one way or another, you know that its meanings are deep," says one of Louisiana's most famous psychics.

Perhaps that is why the fleur is used by so many businesses and restaurants as part of their iconography. Today, in Louisiana and along the Gulf Coast, you'll find the fleur on the sides of trucks, on neon signs, painted on wood in rural markets, in corporate logos, and in the names of thousands of businesses. The symbol has been adopted as a source of pride and, perhaps, luck for those who place it on the doors of their establishments or use it as their "public face."

Not long ago, the NFL tried to claim that the use of the fleur de lis violated established trademarks. One of the world's most powerful organizations felt it owned all rights to the symbol. You can only imagine how that went over in South Louisiana. They say we're a laid-back group, but just try and take our fleur from us. "Not gonna happen. Never." Needless to say, the NFL quickly backed down.

The fleur had won the day again.

Lagniappe is a Creole term that means "a little extra." It's like a baker's dozen - when a good customer receives 13 pastries instead of 12 as a measure of good will. With this in mind, we thought you might enjoy a little extra. Following are some fun facts that you might not know about the fleur de lis. For more, go to our website, www.fleur-de-lis.com/thebook.

The fleur de lis is used as a symbol by the Boy Scouts because the traditional compass used the fleur to indicate True North. True North for a scout was supposed to be his moral compass. That "moral compass" has come into question in recent years as the national association has suffered contention in its ranks regarding the acceptance of some scouts.

The seal of the city of Louisville, Kentucky includes the fleur de lis because the settlement - like Louisiana itself - was named after King Louis of France. The flag of St. Louis, Missouri, originally a French settlement in colonial Louisiana, bears a fleur de lis.

The city of Florence, one of the great cities of the Italian Renaissance, bears a distinct fleur as its symbol - and has since at least the 11th century. This is about the same time that the Merovingian French king adopted the symbol. The symbol was so treasured by Florentine society that when Napoleon tried to change it - (after all, it was also the symbol of the Bourbon dynasty that he replaced and was trying to obliterate) - resistance was so great that he withdrew his demand.

Joan of Arc carried the fleur on a banner into battle. A bronze statue of the "Maid of Orleans" was gifted to the city of New Orleans by the French government. It stands in a triangle on Decatur Street across from the French Market. If you look at the banner, will you see a fleur de lis?

Emerald wallpaper with golden fleur de lis on it - said to be an exact copy of the original - lines the upper tier of the mirrored walls of world-famous Galatoire's Restaurant on Bourbon Street.

On Bourbon Street alone we found over 333 fleur de lis between Iberville and St. Anne Street. Can you?

To discover maps with the fleur on them, visit the Pensacola Historical Society. Old maps in their collection provide insight into the important symbolism of the fleur for those who explored the New World.

LAGNIAPPE • ??

The ninth Steamboat NATCHEZ is the last authentic steamboat to ply the Mississippi River. During the riverboat's heyday, over 3,000 paddle wheelers traveled from New Orleans to Baton Rouge, Shreveport, Natchez, St. Louis and to hundreds of smaller ports up to Illinois and along the Ohio River. Mark Twain would become a steamboat pilot to quench his thirst for adventure.

Today steamboats may be a dying breed but the fleur de lis, a symbol used on furniture, utensils, and the finest china on these "floating palaces," has never gone out of style. Once used on maps and compasses to indicate "True North," the fleur represents a fundamental, natural, mysterious element that helps direct the curious to their metaphorical "True North."

So what does the fleur really mean? For an enslaved African with the fleur branded into their flesh it meant subjugation. Alternatively, for those of African descent, the fact that the symbol originated in Africa is a source of pride. For royalty, it connected the King with divinity. For today's denizens of South Louisiana it often means resilience, family, hope, luck, and home.

In 2011 the New Orleans Saints won the Superbowl. After the stunning defeats that South Louisiana and the Gulf Coast encountered a decade ago during Hurricane Katrina, the win became a psychological turning point for a region that had suffered collective PTSD.

After over four decades of "bad luck," a team that only die-hards believed in became a team that inspired "true believers." Victory after stunning victory, the people of the region stood and roared. Amazed, in a frenzy of excitement, they cheered "the boys" on. It was said that "pigs would fly" and hell would freeze before the Saints ever won the Superbowl. Well, pigs flew. With the overwhelming support of an America that had come to love New Orleans by almost losing it, the underdogs snatched victory for a downtrodden people.

And so they celebrated. They did so like no others before them. They festivaled with food, danced in the streets to jazz, and mixed it all up with Mardi Gras. Some are still celebrating.

Before every cheering fan, on every float, on waving pennants, etched into go-cups, on jerseys worn by every creature on two and four legs, a fleur de lis found purchase. Just when the battle needed most to be won, this mysterious symbol - a symbol that helped define civilization - helped a people shake off the repercussions of a mighty, deadly storm and its depressing residue.

It was time to move on. It was time to finish rebuilding. It was time to heal. Is it any surprise, after all, that the fleur would symbolically lead us toward a more fruitful recovery and point us to toward tomorrow with its steady compass pointing to a metaphorical, if not divine, True North?

FINALE

EPILOQUE

Today the message of the fleur de lis - that of of divine hope and resilience - is being used for causes intended to invigorate the arts and enrich underprivileged communities.

Angela Carville Fluker inspired charitable work in the name of the fleur de lis. Active in her community in life, her death would give birth to the Fleur De Lis fund for art education in Louisiana public schools and to help communities as far away as El Salvador to spark economic self-sufficiency. Her story, like the story of so many people who were touched by the fleur, lives on today within the pages of this book and through the good deeds accomplished by those who believe in the power of *charity, grace and hope*.

RESILIENCE AND HOPE

ABOUT US

Casey Delmont Johnson first envisioned a book about the fleur de lis in 2014 when he became enamored by the beauty and mystery of the symbol. A philosophy and art history major who graduated from Louisiana State University, he researched the fleur and began to discover hidden meanings. Mr. Johnson's goal was to renew interest in the fleur and to encourage others to discover the sacred symbols around them.

In 2015, Mr. Johnson approached New Orleans' leading historical "color analyst," photographer and author Morgan Molthrop, to write and provide images for this book. Mr. Molthrop is the Chief Creative Officer of Custom New Orleans, the city's leading destinations management company. He is the author of ARTIST SPACES, NEW ORLEANS, ANDREW JACKSON'S PLAYBOOK: 15 STRATEGIES FOR SUCCESS, and LOVE: NEW ORLEANS. He is currently working on his fifth book, FUNKY TOWN. He owns Barataria Press, which has partnered with Fleur-de-lis.com on this project.

INTERACTIVE CONTENT

www.fleur-de-lis.com

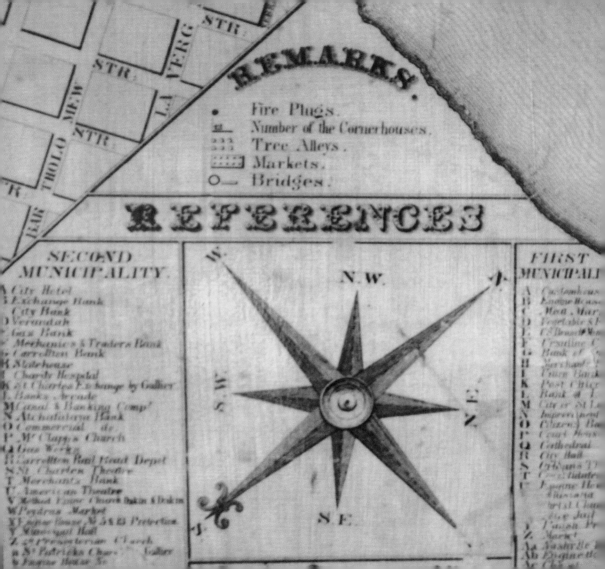